CREATIVE COLOURING

ORCHARD

ORCHARD BOOKS
First published in Great Britain in 2016 by The Watts Publishing Group
1 3 5 7 9 10 8 6 4 2

©2016 The Pokémon Company International.
©1995-2016 Nintendo/Creatures Inc./GAME FREAK inc. TM, ®, and character names are trademarks of Nintendo.

A CIP catalogue record for this book is available from the British Library.

ISBN 978 1 40834 994 6

Printed and bound in Italy

Orchard Books
An imprint of Hachette Children's Group
Part of The Watts Publishing Group Limited
Carmelite House
50 Victoria Embankment
London EC4Y 0DZ

An Hachette UK Company
www.hachette.co.uk

www.hachettechildrens.co.uk

THIS BOOK BELONGS TO

....

....

Welcome to the Pokémon Creative Colouring Book.
Inside these pages are hundreds of Pokémon for you
to find, colour and really make your own.

Relax in the pleasure of creativity and truly
immerse yourself in the Pokémon universe.

Can you spot all of your favourite Pokémon?
Eevee, Jigglypuff, Pikachu, Meowth – they're
all in here. Complete the exciting scenes in
this book and you'll be well on your way to
becoming a true Pokémon expert!

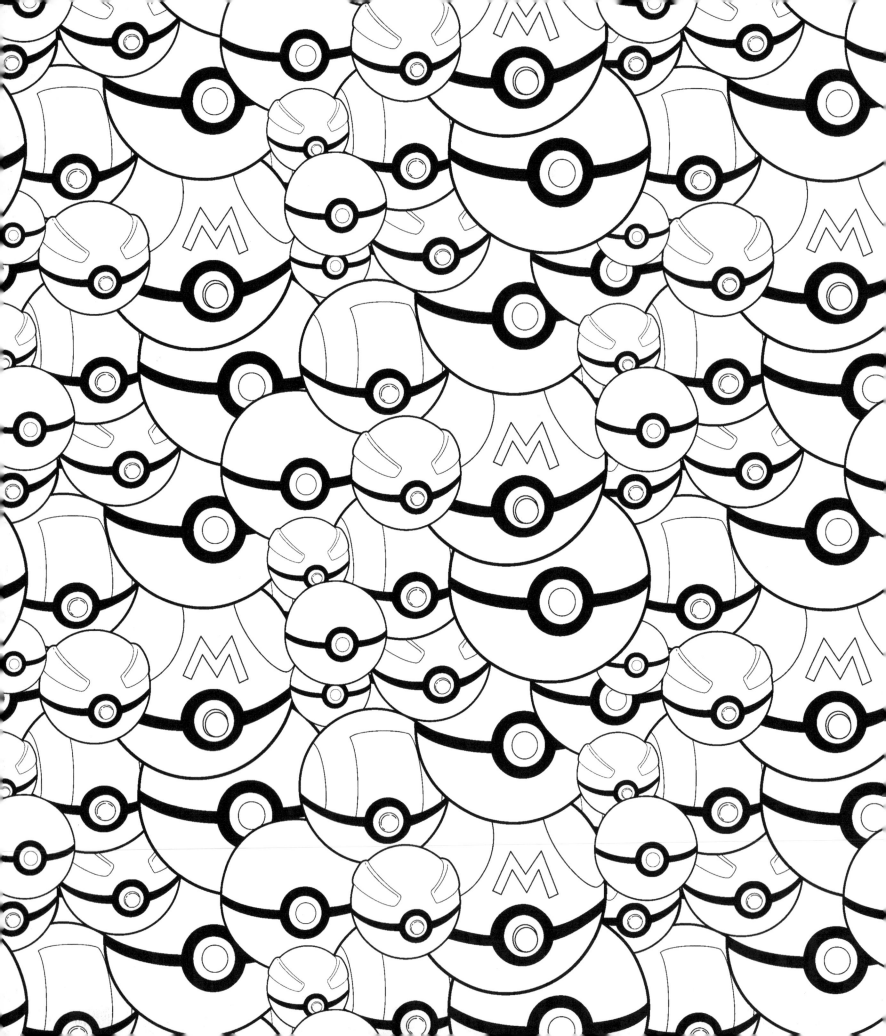

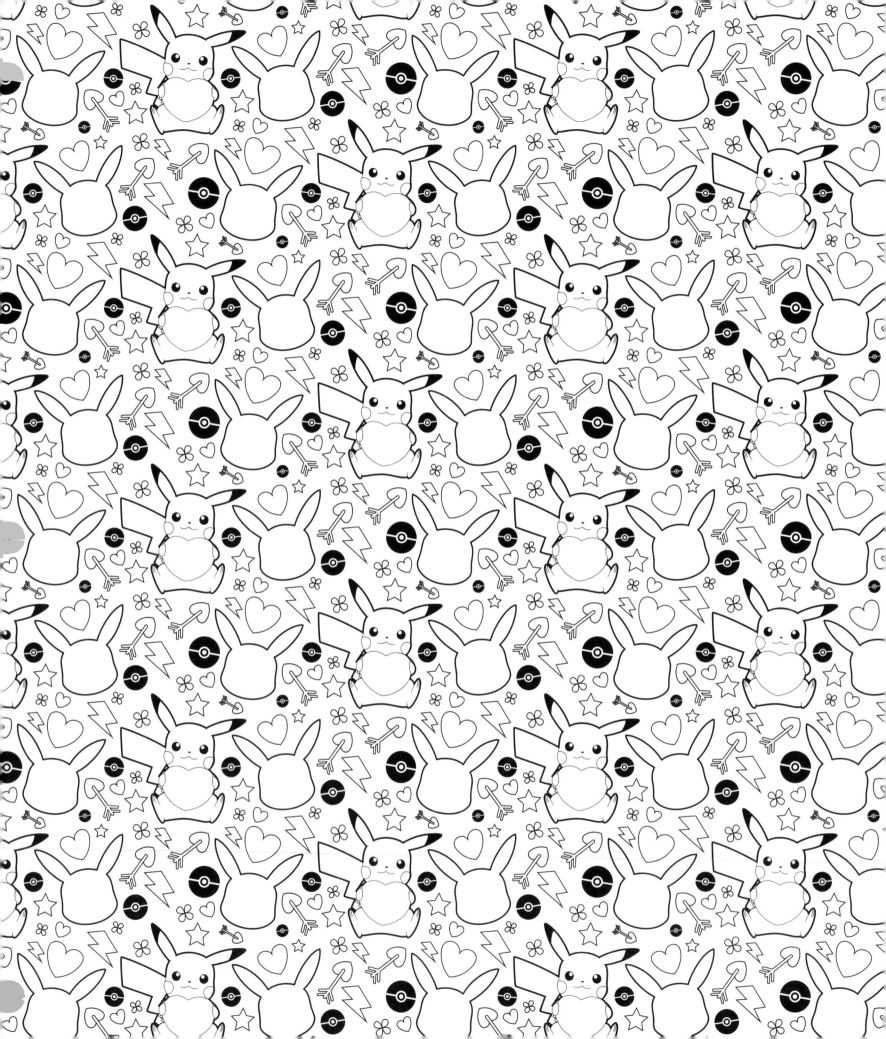

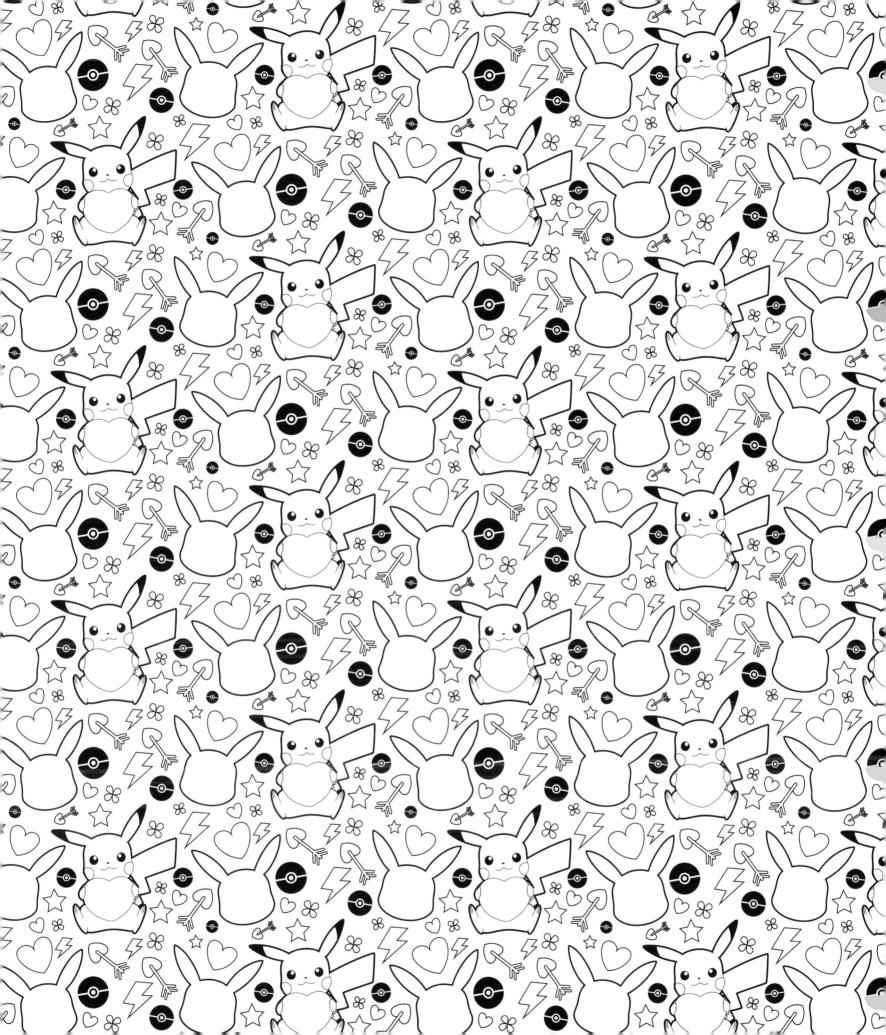